First World War
and Army of Occupation
War Diary
France, Belgium and Germany

59 DIVISION
Divisional Troops
King's Royal Rifle Corps
25th Battalion Pioneers
1 May 1918 - 31 July 1919

WO95/3017/9

The Naval & Military Press Ltd
www.nmarchive.com
Published in association with The National Archives

Published by

The Naval & Military Press Ltd

Unit 10 Ridgewood Industrial Park,

Uckfield, East Sussex,

TN22 5QE England

Tel: +44 (0) 1825 749494

www.naval-military-press.com

www.nmarchive.com

This diary has been reprinted in facsimile from the original. Any imperfections are inevitably reproduced and the quality may fall short of modern type and cartographic standards.

© **Crown Copyright**
Images reproduced by permission of The National Archives, London, England, 2015.

Contents

Document type	Place/Title	Date From	Date To
Heading	WO95/3017/9		
Heading	59th Division 25th Bn King's Roy. Rifle Corps (Pioneers) 1918 May-July 1919		
Heading	25th Garrison Bn King's Royal Rifle Corps War Diary Appendix 1 May 1918		
Heading	59th Division Herewith Royal Corps Of War Diary For The Month Of October 1918		
War Diary	Saulty	01/05/1918	19/05/1918
War Diary	Move	20/05/1918	21/05/1918
War Diary	Verdrel	22/05/1918	31/05/1918
War Diary	Bois D'Olhain	01/06/1918	15/06/1918
War Diary	Bois De Rietz	16/06/1918	16/06/1918
War Diary	Pressy Les Pernes	17/06/1918	17/06/1918
War Diary	Palfart	18/06/1918	18/06/1918
War Diary	Vincly	19/06/1918	09/07/1918
War Diary	Fiefs	10/07/1918	24/07/1918
War Diary	Purple Line Near Ficheux R35+R 36 (51 CSE)	25/07/1918	31/08/1918
War Diary	S'Venant	01/09/1918	05/09/1918
War Diary	La Gorgue	07/09/1918	30/09/1918
Heading	The German Offensive 27th March 1918 General Situation		
War Diary	La Gorgue	01/10/1918	01/10/1918
War Diary	Estaires	02/10/1918	02/10/1918
War Diary	Rouge De Bout	06/10/1918	17/10/1918
War Diary	Lambersart	18/10/1918	18/10/1918
War Diary	Hem	20/10/1918	31/10/1918
Heading	War Diary for The month Of November, 1918.		
War Diary	Hem	01/11/1918	01/11/1918
War Diary	Ramesgnies Chin	10/11/1918	10/11/1918
War Diary	Barry	12/11/1918	16/11/1918
War Diary	Kain	18/11/1918	18/11/1918
War Diary	Templeuve	19/11/1918	19/11/1918
War Diary	Ronchin	20/11/1918	20/11/1918
War Diary	Seclin	21/11/1918	30/11/1918
Heading	War Diary for The month Of December, 1918		
War Diary	Seclin	01/12/1918	07/12/1918
War Diary	Drouvin	10/12/1918	10/12/1918
War Diary	Verdrel	16/12/1918	31/12/1918
Heading	War Diary for The month Of January, 1919		
War Diary	Verdrel	01/01/1919	25/01/1919
War Diary	Dunkirk	26/01/1919	10/03/1919
War Diary	Calais	11/03/1919	31/03/1919
War Diary	Beaumarais	01/04/1919	30/04/1919
War Diary	Beaumarais (near Calais)	01/05/1919	01/05/1919
War Diary	Beaumarais	31/05/1919	31/07/1919
Heading	War Diary No. 2 Provisional Garrison Guard Battalion.		
Miscellaneous	Appendix 1 25th Battn. King's R.R.C. Corps. (P)		
Map	Appendix 1		
Map	Map		
Miscellaneous	Defence Scheme.		

Miscellaneous	No. 2 Provisional (Garr. Guard) Battn. Orders For Defence.
Miscellaneous	Appendix 2
Miscellaneous	Saulty. V2c 30.10. Appendix 3
Miscellaneous	Appendix 4. Stragglers Posts.
Miscellaneous	Appendix 5
Miscellaneous	Appendix 6
Miscellaneous	Appendix 7
Miscellaneous	Appendix 8
Miscellaneous	Appendix 9. Dispositions of Hotchkiss and Lewis Guns.

wo 95 cm
3017/9

59TH DIVISION

25TH BN
KING'S ROY. RIFLE CORPS
(PIONEERS)
1918 MAY – ~~DEC 1918~~
JULY 1919.

FORMED IN FRANCE 1918 MAY

Secret
+
Confidential

25th Garrison Bn
King's Royal Rifle Corps

WAR DIARY

Appendix 1

MAY 1918

late 2nd Prov. G.G. Bn

Headquarters
59th Division

G 112

Herewith Original Copy of
WAR DIARY for the month
of October 1918

R. Underwood Lt Col
Commanding
25 Bn. K.R.R.C.
(P)

31/10/18

CONFIDENTIAL

MAY 1918

WAR DIARY or **INTELLIGENCE SUMMARY**

Army Form C. 2118.

25 Garrison Bn. King's Royal Rifle Corps. late 2nd Prov. G.G. Bn.

Place	Date	Hour	Summary of Events and Information	Remarks and references to Appendices
V8a SAULTY	1/5/18	–	Strength of Battalion. 13 Officers. 849 other ranks. C.O. attended conference at Brigade H.Q. (AVESNES-LE-COMPTE) Chief Instructor training, Lewis Gunnery Officer G.H.Q. line.	Sheet 5/c Appendix 1.
"	2/5/18	"	Officer Commanding Training Cadre (VII Corps Sch.) lectured all officers and N.C.O.'s on the Rifle.	A/C end
"	3/5/18	"	Brigadier General C.G. Williams DSO Commanding 199th Brigade lectured all officers and N.C.O's of the Bn. on "Lessons learned in recent fighting". She work on G.H.Q. line cont'd	A/C end
"	4/5/18	"	199 Brigade Gas Officer inspected Box Respirators of whole Battn.	A/C end
"	5/5/18	"	Reinforcement of 6 officers arrived.	A/C end
"	6/5/18	"	G.O.C. 199 Brigade visited Camp.	A/T.
"	7/5/18	"	Reinforcement of 4 officers arrived. Reserve Army Commander visited Camp.	a/T
"	8/5/18	"	Batt'n for 1st time of Battn. at LAHERLIERE. Work on G.H.Q. line	a/T Appendix 1
"	9/5/18	"	" "	a/T , 1
"	10/5/18	"	Communication Trench in rear of Batt. Sector deepened and firestepped.	a/T , 1
"	11/5/18	"	Communicator Trench – R1 " " deepened.	a/T , 1
"	12/5/18	"	Inspection of Battn. by Commanding Officer. (Sunday)	a/T
"	13/5/18	"	Work and training. 5hrs and 1/2 speeches	a/T
"	14/5/18	"	Work and training	a/T

CONFIDENTIAL

Army Form C. 2118.

WAR DIARY
or
INTELLIGENCE SUMMARY

(Erase heading not required.)

MAY 1918

25th Bn. Kings Royal Rifle Corps.
Cdr. 2nd Bn. G.G. Bn.

Instructions regarding War Diaries and Intelligence Summaries are contained in F.S. Regs., Part II. and the Staff Manual respectively. Title pages will be prepared in manuscript.

Place	Date	Hour	Summary of Events and Information	Remarks and references to Appendices
SAULTY	May 15	—	146th Inf Brigade relieved 199th Brigade. Unit now under the former. VII Corps School training off	V8a. Shut 57c
"	16	—	Cadre left the Brigade	
"	"	—	Conference at Brigade H.Q. (AVESNES LE COMPTE) Commanding Officer attended.	J. Shut 57c
"	"	2.45pm	Battle Stations were manned — an alarm practice. Disposition as in Appendix 1.	App. 1
"	17	—	Work and Training.	
"	18	"	" " Training.	
"	"	"	" Training.	
"	19	"	The I received notice that the Battalion would move on Monday the 20th to Hq	
"	"	"	G.H.Q. Line having been practically completed	
MOVE	20	4am	Battalion marched to LATTRE St QUENTIN. Billeted.	J. 57c.
MOVE	21	4am	Battalion marched to MAGNICOURT. Billeted.	
VERDREL	22	7am	Battalion marched to BOIS D'OHLAIN near VERDREL & encamped in wood.	Q4a 36b
"	23	—	The whole Battalion worked in Camp area.	
"	24	5.30am	Digging of the B.B. Line commenced. (BRUAY - BARLIN) No 1 Sector. 6h.	Shut 36b
"	25	5.30	1 hr training daily	
"	"	"	As above	
"	26	9am	Sunday. Training until 1pm. Inspection, Musketry etc. Designation changed as above.	

CONFIDENTIAL

Army Form C. 2118.

MAY 1918 WAR DIARY
25 Garrison Bn
King's Royal Rifle Corps
INTELLIGENCE SUMMARY
(Erase heading not required.)

Instructions regarding War Diaries and Intelligence Summaries are contained in F. S. Regs., Part II. and the Staff Manual respectively. Title pages will be prepared in manuscript.

Place	Date	Hour	Summary of Events and Information	Remarks and references to Appendices
VERDREL	May 27	—	A.D.M.S. 59th Div. visited Camp. 'A' Co. inspected by Medical Officer of the Div	A
"	28	—	'B' Co inspected by Medical Officer	A
"	29	—	B + C Coys inspected by Medical Officer of Div	A
"	30	—	59th Div. Commander visited Camp	A
"	31	—	Strength today 28 Officers and 909 other ranks, including attached medical Officer and Armourer Sergeant.	A

E. H. Wardrove, Lt Col
Commanding
25th Garr. Bn.
K.R.R. Corps

31/5/18

CONFIDENTIAL
Army Form C. 2118.

JUNE 1918
25th Bn. King's Royal Rifle Corps
WAR DIARY
or
INTELLIGENCE SUMMARY
(Erase heading not required.)

Instructions regarding War Diaries and Intelligence Summaries are contained in F.S. Regs., Part II. and the Staff Manual respectively. Title pages will be prepared in manuscript.

Place	Date 1918	Hour	Summary of Events and Information	Remarks and references to Appendices
BOIS D'OHLAIN	June 1st to Jun 15th		Strength of Unit 28 Officers. 908 other ranks. Administered by 124th Inf Brigade. Work on B.B. Line. (BRUAY to ESTRÉE-CAUCHIE). Programme for each day:- 6 hr's digging task. 1 hr's training a.r.	Q 14b 2.8 Sheet 44b. 5.5
BOIS des RIETZ	16th		Battalion moved to Bois des RIETZ. Hostile air-raid during the night (11pm). 2 casualties wounded. a.r.	T.12.d.3.0. Sheet 44b. H.15.v.16 Sheet 44b.
PRESSY les PERNES	17th		Battalion moved to PRESSY-les-PERNES a.r.	
PALFART.	18th		Battalion moved to PALFART. The unit became disorganised 59th Divisional Concept. a.r.	A 13.v.14 44b
VINCLY	19th		Battalion moved to VINCLY. The unit was administered direct by 59th Divisional a.r.	W.9.15.v.16 Sheet 36 D
	20th		Battalion was re-organised on a 3 Coy basis & was attached to 176 Inf. Brigade for administration a.r.	
	21st		Training commenced. Six hours per day. a.r.	
	24th		The Unit came under orders of 124 Inf. Brigade for Tng. a.r.	
	21st-30th		Training 6 hrs per day. During this period there was a slight epidemic of Influenza. Average number of cases per day was 6. On June 30th 114 Cases were admitted to hospital. a.r. Strength of Unit 29 Officers 936 other ranks	

J.H.Wedderspoon Lt Col
Commanding 25th Bn. R.K.R.Corps.

CONFIDENTIAL

Army Form C. 2118.

WAR DIARY or INTELLIGENCE SUMMARY

25th King's Royal Rifle Corps (Pioneers)

JULY 1918

Instructions regarding War Diaries and Intelligence Summaries are contained in F.S. Regs., Part II. and the Staff Manual respectively. Title pages will be prepared in manuscript.

(Erase heading not required.)

Vol. 3

Place	Date	Hour	Summary of Events and Information	Remarks and references to Appendices
VINCLY	JULY 1st to 3rd	—	Strength of Unit 29 Officers 934 Other ranks. Training for Othr ranks with a view to the occupation of Trenches. The Unit is administered by the 178 Inf: Brigade. aR	1/Map 3CD W 9 + 15
"	4th	—	The Battalion was re-organised as a 3 Company basis in accordance with War Establishment of a Pioneer Battn. aR	
"	5th to 9th	—	Training 6 hrs daily. Quiet period. aR	
"	10th	—	Battalion moved to billets in FIEFS. aR	Sheet 44A & A.28
FIEFS			Battalion moved to FIEFS for administration. aR	
"	11th	—	G.O.C. 59th Division inspected the Battalion. 2nd Lt. A.J. STANDWICK and Lieut F.J. MAGEE Officer reinforcements arrived. Officer Inspector of Baths visited the Bn. and inspected Officers and other ranks who had been reported as "unfit". aR	
"	12th to 15th	—	Battalion carried out usual Infantry training. 6 hrs daily. Quiet period aR	
"	16th	—	The word "Carrier" was eliminated from the designation of the Bn. Usual Infantry training carried out. aR	

CONFIDENTIAL.

Army Form C. 2118.

WAR DIARY or INTELLIGENCE SUMMARY.

25th Bn. King's Royal Rifle Corps (Annex)

(Erase heading not required.)

Instructions regarding War Diaries and Intelligence Summaries are contained in F.S. Regs., Part II. and the Staff Manual respectively. Title pages will be prepared in manuscript.

JULY 1918

Place	Date	Hour	Summary of Events and Information	Remarks and references to Appendices
FIEFS	JULY 17th	—	Training. 7 Officers and 908 Other Ranks who had been re-classified Cat. B.II & B.III proceeded to the Base. aR.	Sheet 44 b A 28
	18th to 21st	—	Battn. carried out Infantry training &c. daily. aR.	
	22nd	—	Lt. J.F. MAGINNIS proceeded to Base, sick. aR.	
	23rd	—	178th Infantry Brigade moved to BARLY AREA. The Battn. was left behind and ordered to proceed under the orders of the 177 Inf. Brigade. aR.	Sheet 51c SE. F.15.
	24th	—	Battn. carried out training. aR	
PURPLE LINE near FICHEUX R 35 & R 36 (51c S.E)	25th	12.45 pm	The Battalion was moved by motor lorries to the vicinity of the PURPLE LINE. "B" + "C" Companies relieved the Battn., P.P.C.L.I. of the 3rd Canadian Division in the PURPLE LINE at 10.45 p.m. on the 25th. "A" Company proceeded to WAILLY HUTS and were attached to the 1997 Tunnelling Company (Canadians) for work. aR.	Appendix I.
	26th + 27th		Very quiet days in the line. No shelling. aR.	

CONFIDENTIAL

Army Form C. 2118.

JULY 1918. 25th Bn: King's Royal Rifle Corps. (P)

WAR DIARY
or
INTELLIGENCE SUMMARY.
(Erase heading not required.)

Instructions regarding War Diaries and Intelligence Summaries are contained in F.S. Regs., Part II. and the Staff Manual respectively. Title pages will be prepared in manuscript.

Place	Date	Hour	Summary of Events and Information	Remarks and references to Appendices
PURPLE LINE	July 28th to 31st	—	Quiet period. 6 Officers reinforcements received. Strength of Unit 31 Officers Other Ranks 813 including attached a.R. Total evacuated for period in the line :- 1 other rank wounded.	Appendix I

R. Underwood Lt Col
Commanding
25th Bn KRR Corps (P)

31st July 1918

Army Form C. 2118.

25th King's Royal Rifle Corps (Trench)
WAR DIARY
or
INTELLIGENCE SUMMARY.
CONFIDENTIAL.

(Erase heading not required.)

AUGUST.

Place	Date	Hour	Summary of Events and Information	Remarks and references to Appendices
PURPLE LINE	August 1st	-	Strength of Unit 32 Officers 812 Other ranks. aJ.	R30a 8.35 Sheet 57c. S.W.
	1st to 4th	-	Quiet period. Companies at work on communication trenches in forward system. On night of 2/3rd August 177 & 178 Infantry Brigades relieved 176 Inf. Brigade. aJ	9 H 4
	8th	-	On the night of August 8th/9th 176 Inf. Brigade relieved 177 Inf. Brigade & supported sector aJ	
	9th to 17th	-	Quiet period. aJ	
	17/18th	-	147 Inf. Brigade relieved 178 Inf. Brigade in Right sub-sector. aJ	
	18th to 21st	-	Quiet period aJ	
	21/22	-	178 Inf. Brigade relieved 3rd Guards Brigade in the Rt. of Lived Sector. 'C' Company cut wire and hedged thereto at S5 b + d. Sheet 51b. S.W. aJ. Battalion in reserve occupied Purple System. The 24th hr.	LENS. 11 G.4. 36a Sheet N.14.C.
FICHEUX	23	-	Battalion proceeded to Sauty & bivouacked for the night. Arrived 1 am in aJ 5th Division was relieved by the 52nd Div for 3.30 am 25th aJ Battalion proceeded to QUERNES. Arrived	
	24	-	aJ	
	25th 26 27th	-	Quiet time. Battalion in billets. aJ 59th Division relieved the 44th Div & MERVILLE AREA. The Battalion entrained & proceeded to ASYLUM, ST VENANT. aJ	Sheet 36 a P. 9.6. +d.
	28th to 3pm	-	Quiet period. Enemy retired 3 or 4 kilometers. Companies working to evacuate and repair trenches. Strength of Unit 29 Off. 812 Other Ranks. aJ	

Command 25th K.R.R. Corps.

CONFIDENTIAL

25th Bn. King's Royal Rifle Corps (Pnr)

Army Form C. 2118.

25 KRRC
9/12 5

SEPTEMBER 1915
WAR DIARY
INTELLIGENCE SUMMARY.
(Erase heading not required.)

Instructions regarding War Diaries and Intelligence Summaries are contained in F. S. Regs., Part II. and the Staff Manual respectively. Title pages will be prepared in manuscript.

Place	Date	Hour	Summary of Events and Information	Remarks and references to Appendices
ST VENANT.	Sept. 1st to 4th		Strength of Battalion:- 29 Officers 812 other ranks. aqf All Companies employed on roads between Vieraut and Calonne under orders of C.R.E. 39th Division, filling mine craters etc. aqf	Sheet Sha P 9 a
	5th		All Companies moved forward. A Coy L Marcis Coy, R 11 c, B Coy to La Gorgue and C Coy to Frove Fav. R 22 a. aqf	Sheet Neuve-Chapelle
			Battalion Headquarters moved forward to La Gorgue. aqf	L.55a Central Neuve-Chapelle
LA GORGUE	7th		Battalion was employed on road repair, drainage etc. Guer Favrel. B Coy moved to M 14/23.2 7/9/15. aqf	
	7th to 27th			
	28th		Companies were re-arranged for work under orders of Officers Commanding 467, 469, and 470 Field Coys. R.E. aqf	
	29th		Work as usual. Quiet day. aqf	
	30th	7.30 am	39th Division in conjunction with the 19th Division attacked the enemy. 29 Buccaneer Brigade was entry line running from N 13 d.5.8 to N 19 c 35.10. During the month, there was 1 battle casualty (1 Off. wounded 30/9/15.) A second-in-command, a Quartermaster and 4 other officers reinforcements reported for duty. Four officers were struck off strength. Strength of Battalion 31 Officers 804 other ranks. aqf	Sheet AUBERS 36 S.W.

R. Whellurn Lt. Col
Commanding 25th Bn. KRRC (Pnr)

Printer's Copy

Masse
with
Macmath

1918. ××
Chapter 1.

The German Offensive

27th March 1918.

General Situation

5) checks front div.
10)
5 Order of battle of GAR

Add Wilson

pp 12
checked JS 5/2/55

CONFIDENTIAL

WAR DIARY

INTELLIGENCE SUMMARY

(Erase heading not required.)

Army Form C. 2118.

25th Bn. King's Royal Rifle Corps

OCTOBER. 1918

Instructions regarding War Diaries and Intelligence Summaries are contained in F. S. Regs., Part II. and the Staff Manual respectively. Title pages will be prepared in manuscript.

Place	Date	Hour	Summary of Events and Information	Remarks and references to Appendices
La Gorgue	Oct 1st	—	Strength of Battn: 31 Officers 804 other ranks. a/f.	L.34.d & 5.5 Sheet 36a
Estaires	Oct 2nd	—	Division advanced. Battalion Hd. Quarter Company moved to ESTAIRES. The three companies A, B & C was attached to the 467, 469 & 470 Field Coys: R.E. and moved forward with them. a/f.	L.29 + 30 Sheet 36a
Rouge de Bout	Oct 5th	—	Quiet period from the 2nd inst. Battalion again moved forward to the lines to ROUGE de BOUT a/f	H.31.a.5.8 Sheet 36
" "	Oct 6th to Oct 14th	—	Quiet period. Companies at work at mine craters and road repairs. a/f	
" "	Oct 14th	—	Battalion HQ moved forward to La Vesée Post. a/f.	I.19.b.58 Sheet L.N.W
Lambersart	Oct 18th	—	Battalion HQ moved forward to tiles works LAMBERSART. K.19.C.5.5. a/f. See 36 N.E	
Hem	Oct 20th	—	Battalion HQ moved forward to HEM. a/f. During the divisional advance, the three companies of the Battalion were engaged on road and bridge repairs in the divisional area. Two important bridges at K.20.d.5.2 (36.NE) and at L.29.b.6.9 were constructed. a/f	G.25.2.8.8 Sheet 37.
"	to Oct 31st	—	Quiet period in rear at HEM. Strength of Bn: Officers 34, o.r. 815 a/f 1 Battle Casualty during the month. 1 o.r. wounded	

P. Shillard Lt Col
Comm. as. dy 25th Bn. K.R.R. Corps. (P)

T. 70.

To,
Headquarters,
59th. Division.

Herewith War Diary for the month of November, 1918.

29/11/18.

..........................Lt.-Col.
Commanding 25th.Bn.K.R.R.Corps.(P.)

NOVEMBER 1918.

25th Bn. K.R.R. CORPS. (Pnrs)

CONFIDENTIAL

WAR DIARY or INTELLIGENCE SUMMARY.

Army Form C. 2118.

(Erase heading not required.)

Instructions regarding War Diaries and Intelligence Summaries are contained in F. S. Regs., Part II. and the Staff Manual respectively. Title pages will be prepared in manuscript.

Place	Date	Hour	Summary of Events and Information	Remarks and references to Appendices
HEM	Nov 1st	—	Strength of Unit: 34 Officers, 815 Other Ranks. Unit under 59th Div.; XI Corps. Fifth Army. Companies working on road repairing.	G.26 Sheet 37
RAMESGNIES CHIN	10th	—	The Unit moved into billets at RAMESGNIES CHIN. at.	T 25 a Sheet 37.
BARRY	12th	—	The Battalion moved to BARRY, and worked on the railroad in the vicinity of the Station for four days, removing broken rails and filling mine craters. at.	Q 35 Sheet 37.
BARRY	16th	—	Under Army Reorganization, the XI Corps and 59th Div. came under the orders of the First Army. at.	
KAIN	18th	—	The Battalion moved to KAIN. at	O.5 Sheet 37
TEMPLEUVE	19th	—	The Battalion moved to TEMPLEUVE. at.	H 33 Sheet 37
RONCHIN	20th	—	The Battalion moved to RONCHIN. at	Q 29 Sheet 36
SECLIN	21st	—	The Battalion moved to SECLIN. at	V 30. Sheet 36
"	30th	—	Battalion in billets at SECLIN. Strength of Battn. 31 Officers, 741 Other Ranks. 1 Officer reinforcement reported during the month. There were no battle casualties during the month. at.	

Sherwood. Lt Col
Commanding 25th Bn. KRR Corps.

Headquarters
59th Division

A119

Herewith war diary for the month of December 1918.

Thos H Morgan
Major
Comma'dg
25th Bn K R R Corps.

9/1/19

25th Bn KRR Corps (1?)

DECEMBER 1918.

WAR DIARY

INTELLIGENCE SUMMARY.

Army Form C. 2118.

CONFIDENTIAL

25 KRR C

Place	Date	Hour	Summary of Events and Information	Remarks and references to Appendices
SECLIN	1/12/18	-	Strength of Unit :- 31 Officers 441 O.R's. Unit resting in Billets.	V.30 Sheet 36 a.f.
SECLIN.	7/12/18	-	Unit moved into Huts at DROUVIN. a.f.	K.4.c Sheet 44.b Near St Pol LENS. 11.
DROUVIN	10/12/18	-	'B' Coy. moved by busses to LIGNY-St-FLOCHEL to assist in construction of XI Corps Concentration Camp. a.f.	
VERDREL	16/12/18	-	Remainder of Battalion moved to Camp at VERDREL. a.f.	Q.15.c O.9. Sheet 44.b
VERDREL	16/12/18 31/12/18	-	Unit engaged in Salvage Work in the vicinity of the Camp. Party of 1 Officer + 50 O.R's engaged in salvage work at Ablain-St-Nazaire. a.f. Strength of Unit :- 29 Officers + 479 O.R's	X.10 Sheet 44.3

Wm Thompson
Major
Commanding
25.B. KRR Corps. 1?

T. 141.

TO,
　　Headquarters,
　　　　59th. Division.

　　　Herewith War Diary for the month of January, 1919.

　　　　　　　　　　　　　　　　　　P. Thirlwood Lt.-Col.
31/1/19.　　　　　Commanding 25th. Bn. K.R.R. Corps. (P.)

JANUARY. 1919
25th King's Royal Rifle Corps. (Pnr.)

CONFIDENTIAL.
Army Form C. 2118.

WAR DIARY
INTELLIGENCE SUMMARY.
(Erase heading not required.)

Instructions regarding War Diaries and Intelligence Summaries are contained in F. S. Regs., Part II. and the Staff Manual respectively. Title pages will be prepared in manuscript.

Place	Date	Hour	Summary of Events and Information	Remarks and references to Appendices
VERDREL	1/1/19 to 25/1/19	—	Strength of Battalion. 29 Officers. 649 Other Ranks. of. Unit engaged on Salvage Work in the area near the Camp. 'B' Company at Lgny St Flochel near St Pol, assisting in constructing XI Corps Concentration Camp. 'B' Coy rejoined Bath on Jany 23rd in preparation for move. of	Sheet 44b Q15c.o.9.
	23/1/19		Battalion entrained at NOEUX-LES-MINES of.	Sheet 44b L.13
DUNKIRK.	24/1/19		Battalion arrived at DUNKIRK, attached to Lines of Communication at	
	25/1/19 to 31/1/19		Battalion engaged on erecting & constructing demobilisation Camps at Dunkirk. of.	
			Strength of Unit 25 Officers 455 Other Ranks at	

[signature]
Commanding
25B KRR Corps. Pnr.

Army Form C. 2118.

WAR DIARY
or
INTELLIGENCE SUMMARY.
(Erase heading not required.)

25th Bn. K.R.R. Corps (e)

WO 10

Place	Date	Hour	Summary of Events and Information	Remarks and references to Appendices
DUNKIRK.	1/9 to 28/9		Strength. 25 Officers 442 O.R. At work with R.E's building Demobilization Camps.	
"	7/9		Received drafts from 11th & 12th Bns. K.R.R. Corps (10 Officers 300 O.R.)	
DUNKIRK.	28/9		Strength 30 Officers 504 O.R.	

R. Shirwood.............Lt-Col.
Commanding 25th Battn. K.R.R. Corps
(Pioneers)

Army Form C. 2118.

WAR DIARY
or
INTELLIGENCE SUMMARY.
(Erase heading not required.)

Instructions regarding War Diaries and Intelligence Summaries are contained in F. S. Regs., Part II. and the Staff Manual respectively. Title pages will be prepared in manuscript.

Place	Date	Hour	Summary of Events and Information	Remarks and references to Appendices
DUNKIRK	1-3-19 to 10-3-19		Strength 501. Erecting Nissen Huts in Mardyck Demob. Camps. Moved by train to Beau Marias near Calais.	
CALAIS	11/3/19 to		Guard Duties in Beau Marias & Fontinette Areas.	
CALAIS	31/3/19		Strength 909.	

.... Lt.-Col.
Commanding 25th Battn. K.R.R. Corps
(Pioneers)

25th Bn. K.R.R. Corps (P)

Army Form C. 2118.

25TH BN.
KING'S
ROYAL RIFLE CORPS.

No. ....
Date. ....

WAR DIARY
or
INTELLIGENCE SUMMARY.
(Erase heading not required.)

Instructions regarding War Diaries and Intelligence Summaries are contained in F. S. Regs., Part II. and the Staff Manual respectively. Title pages will be prepared in manuscript.

Place	Date	Hour	Summary of Events and Information	Remarks and references to Appendices
BEAUMARIS	1/4/19		Strength 976.	
			Guard duties, P.O.W. Escorts &c in CALAIS AREA.	
BEAUMARIS	30/4/19		Strength 1197.	

.... Lt.-Col.
Commanding 25th Batn. K.R.R. Corps
(Pioneers)

Army Form C. 2118.

2/356
2-6-19

25TH BN.,
KING'S
ROYAL RIFLE CORPS.

No. ....
Date ....

WAR DIARY
or
INTELLIGENCE SUMMARY.
(Erase heading not required.)

Place	Date	Hour	Summary of Events and Information	Remarks and references to Appendices
BEAUMARAIS. (near Calais)	1/5/19.		Strength. 24 Officers 1190 Other Ranks. Guard Duties, Prisoner of War Escorts etc., at Calais Fortresses area Beaumarais.	
BEAUMARAIS	31/5/19.		Strength. 35 Officers 1021 Other Ranks.	

G. Whitehead. Lt.-Col.
Commanding 25th Battn. K.R.R. Corps
(Pioneers)

Army Form C. 2118.

25TH BATTN., KING'S ROYAL RIFLE CORPS (PIONEERS).

WAR DIARY
or
INTELLIGENCE SUMMARY.
(Erase heading not required.)

Instructions regarding War Diaries and Intelligence Summaries are contained in F. S. Regs., Part II. and the Staff Manual respectively. Title pages will be prepared in manuscript.

Place	Date	Hour	Summary of Events and Information	Remarks and references to Appendices
BEAUMARIS	1/6/19		Strength Officers 35. Other Ranks 1032.	
			Guard duties in Beaumaris, Jubilee & Lidia Areas	
	17/6/19		"E" Company to Jingham (Guard duties on G.H.Q. Lakes Dumps)	
	23/6/19		"B" Company to Bomdonj (Guard duties on G.H.Q. Lakes Dumps)	
BEAUMARIS	30/6/19		Strength Officers 30. Other Ranks 931.	

Richards, Lt.-Col.
Commanding 25th Batn. K.R.R. Corps.
(Pioneers.)

Army Form C. 2118.

25TH BATTN.
KING'S ROYAL
RIFLE CORPS
(PIONEERS).

No.....................
Date...................

WAR DIARY
or
INTELLIGENCE SUMMARY.
(Erase heading not required.)

Instructions regarding War Diaries and Intelligence
Summaries are contained in F. S. Regs., Part II.
and the Staff Manual respectively. Title pages
will be prepared in manuscript.

Place	Date	Hour	Summary of Events and Information	Remarks and references to Appendices
BEAUMARAIS.	1-7-19.		Strength 30 Officers. 951 Other Ranks.	
			Guard Duties in Calais Area.	
			"B" Company at BOURBOURG (Guard Duties on Ammunition Dumps).	
			"C" Company at ZENEGHEM (Guard Duties on G.H.Q. Salvage Installation).	
BEAUMARAIS.	31-7-19.		Strength 30 Officers. 912 Other Ranks.	

...................................Major.
Commanding 25th, Battn.K.R.R.Corps.(P).

Waldegrave

No. 2 Provisional Garrison Guard Battalion.

DEFENCE SCHEME.

Appendix I

25th Batt'n King's R... Corps (E).

PROVISIONAL ORDERS ... ...

... 1918.

Ref. (..ap to 1:...
..:...

I. DISPOSITIONS:- "B" Coy from ..1.b.85.50. to ....5.d.1.5.(road inclusive)

C.H.Q. at ..25.d.1.0.

"C" Coy from ..1.b.50.80. to ..36.a.75.00.(road inclusive)

C.H.Q. at ..1.b.50.50.

467 Field Coy R.E., from ..25.d.05.70. to ..25.c.2.5.

H..Coy 25th K.. Rifles R.36.d.3.0. to ..25.b.1.5.

470 Field Coy R.E. from R.25.b.1.5. to R.19.c.5.0. Man both Purple Front Line and Immediate Support.

II. ACTION ON RECEIPT OF BATTLE ORDERS.
Companies will man battle stations; 2 Runners from each of "B" & "C" Coys and one from each of 467 & 470 Field Coys R.E. will report to Bn. H.Q. R.30.a.55.40.

"B" & "C" Coys will each send a Lewis Gun Section with Gun to report to Bn. H.Q.

III. METHOD OF DEFENCE.
The Purple Line must be held at all costs. In the event of a break through of the Front Line by the enemy, the principal object of the troops in this line will be the collection of Stragglers and re-organising them into fighting units.

IV. STRAGGLERS POSTS.
Stragglers' Posts will be formed at every spot where a road or track crosses the Purple Line. No unwounded or slightly wounded man will be allowed to proceed to the rear. Stragglers will be re-organised in Platoons & Companies and used as immediate reinforcements. Numbers of stragglers so collected will be reported to Bn. H.Q. every hour.

V. LOCATION OF SUPPLIES ETC.
WATER...Well at R.36.c.4.9.
S.A.A.. 50.000rds Bn. H.Q. R.30.a.55.40.
       20.000rds "B" Coy R.Q.R.25.d.1.0.
       20.000rds "C" Coy R.Q.1.b.50.50.
R.A.P...At R.30.a.7.4.

SYSTEM OF ENEMY ADVANCE.
The methods being adopted to hold up the advance of the enemy in the enclosed country in Flanders should make full use of every building, hedge, or piece of broken ground etc. The defensive dispositions must be concealed. Definite lines of defence should be dug in rear, but houses & buildings etc which exists in front of these lines must be held to the last, and must not be evacuated even when the flanks are turned. Every care must be taken to conceal new holding posts and no movements should be seen. The enemy system of advance is to dribble forward into farm buildings, houses, broken ground etc.and to bring flanking fire to bear on our men occupying hastily dug and very visible trenches in the open.

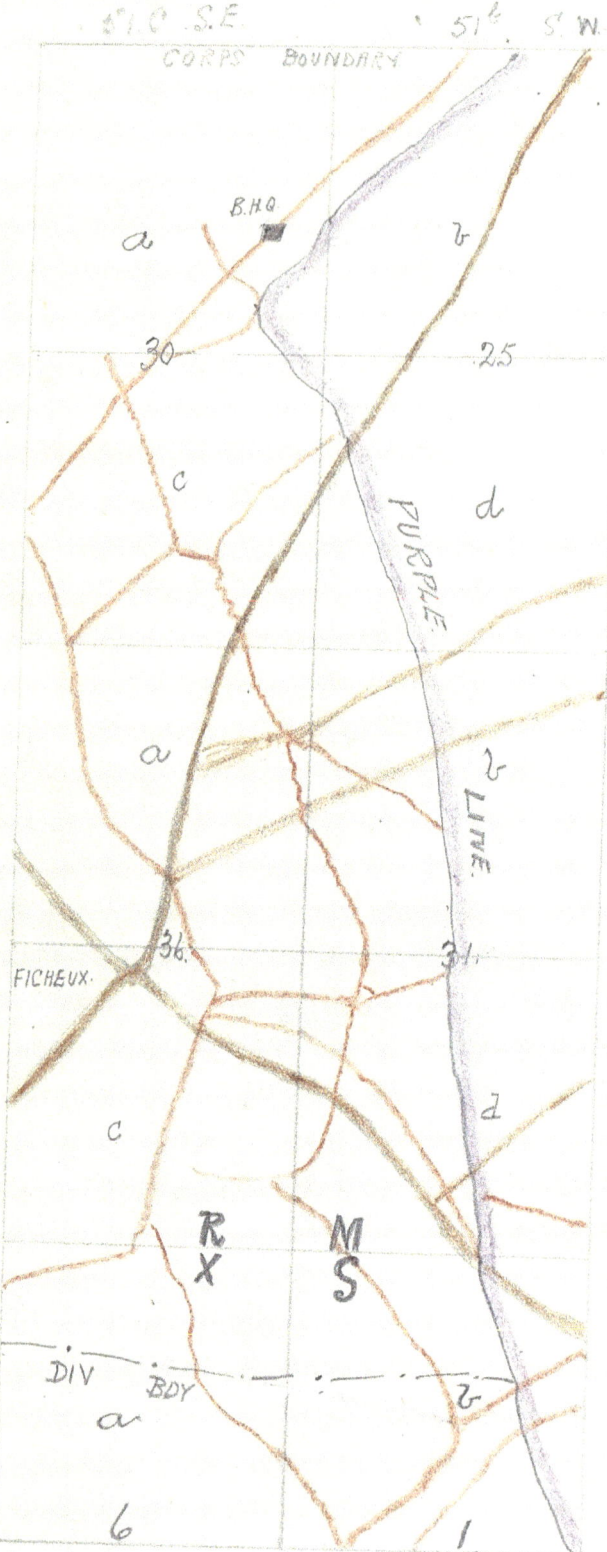

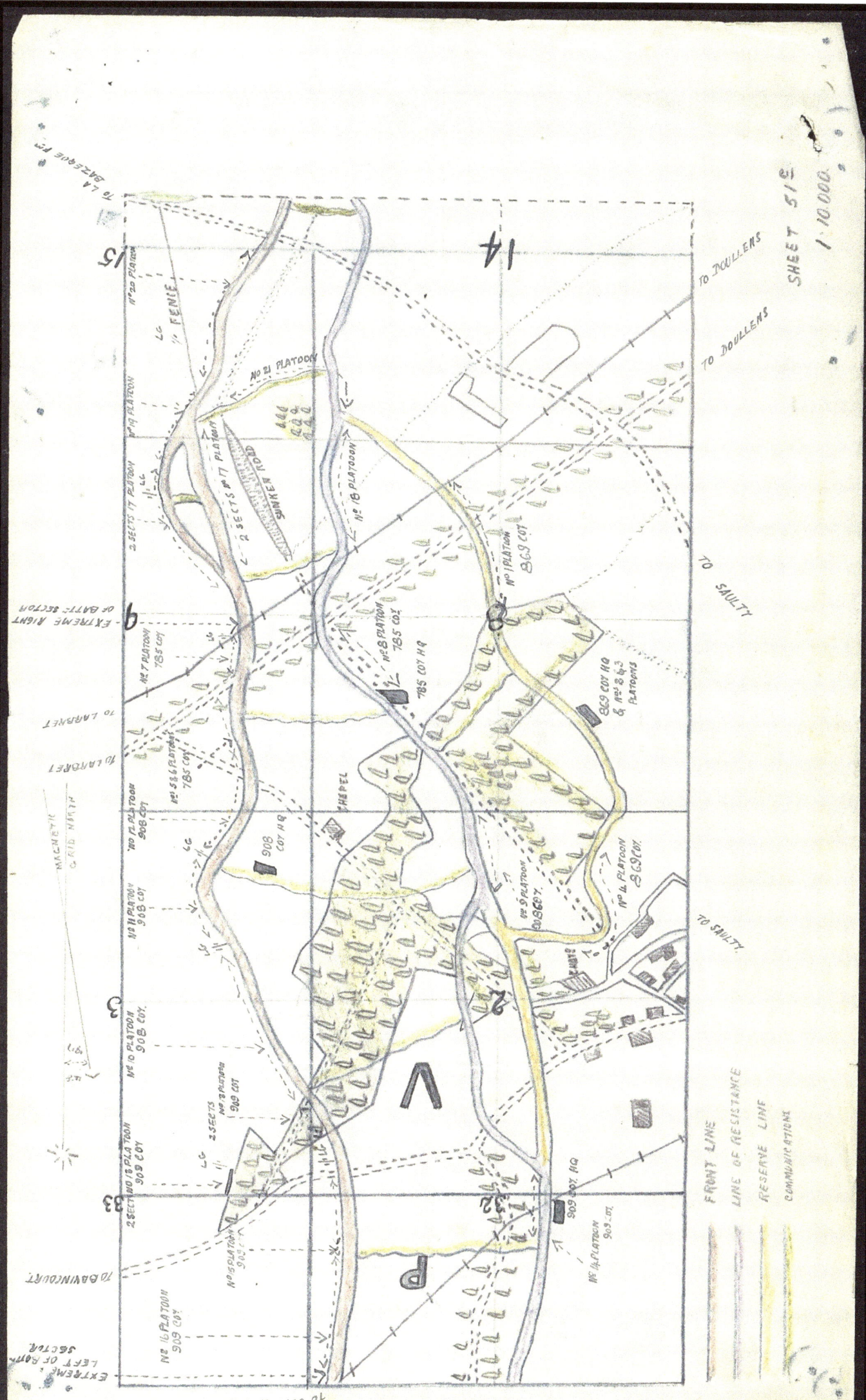

Contents.

Defence Scheme.

Distribution.

Appendices.

1. Action by Platoons of 147 & 176 Labour Coys. on receipt of order to man Battle Positions.
2. Supplies, Water, and Rations.
3. Supplies. S.A.A.
4. Stragglers' Posts.
5. Action by Rt. & Lft. Companies in the event of the withdrawal by troops on our Flanks.
6. Notes on Dispositions of Companies in the Line.
7. Rations for 147 & 176 Labour Coys. *deleted*
8. Methods of holding up an advance.
9. Dispositions of Hotchkiss & Lewis Guns.

Appendix 1.

Action by the Platoons of 147 and 176 Labour Companies on receipt of orders to man Battle Stations.

1. The Platoons will take up Battle Positions as shewn on Map F. When in position, a runner will be sent to Bn. H.Q. with a note to that effect. He will also bring a complete nominal roll of the men of his Company.

2. A runner to be attached to Bn. H.Q. will be sent there as soon as the trench is occupied.

    Deleted

No.2 Provisional (Garr.Guard) Batt'n.

Orders for Defence.

1. Method of holding the Line.

    (a) Each Bn. will hold tactical features in strength. The gaps between them will be held lightly, or even only patrolled. In either case, touch must be kept with the troops on either flank.

    B. The front line will be the line of resistance; the second line will be the support line, and the third line the reserve line.

2. Dispositions of Batt'n.

    (a) This will be as shewn on Map F.
    Notes re dispositions on Appendix 6.

    (b) The additional platoons from 147 Labour Coy. and 176 Labour Coy. will be known as 17, 18, 19, 20, 21 platoons, the two former from 147 Coy, and the three letter from 176 Coy.

3. Action by these platoons on receipt of orders to Man Battle Positions is given in Appendix 1.

4. S.A.A.   Arrangements for the supply of S.A.A. are given in Appendix 3.

5. Stragglers' Posts.   Instructions regarding Stragglers' Posts are given in Appendix 4.

6. Action by Right & Left Companies in case of withdrawal by troops on either flank in Appendix 5.

Appendix 2.

Water.   Two 50 Gall. Tanks.
           166 Petrol Tins.

Rations.   1,000.

           All above at Bn. H.Q.

                        V2 c   30. 10.

Appendix 3.

SAULTY.   V 2 c   30. 10.

100,000 rounds.

On receipt of orders to Man Battle Positions, 869 Coy. will detail carrying parties to form Ammunition Dumps at C.H.Q's of 909, 908, 785, 1/AN, 1/76 Coys.

5,000 rds. to each Coy.

Appendix 4.

Stragglers' Posts.

1. The Strong Point Post provided by 909 Coy. at V 3 a 40 90 will collect all stragglers approaching their west front and use them as reinforcements for the Companies in the Line.

2. 869 Coy. will form a stragglers' post at Road Junc. in V 9 a. 1 N.C.O. and 8. Stragglers will be collected & escorted to 785 Coy. and used as reinforcements.

3. 1 N.C.O. and 8 men from 869 Coy. will form a Stragglers Post at Road Junction at U 6 C 0.4.

All stragglers will be collected and placed in the nearest defended locality. Slightly wounded men will not be allowed to proceed to the rear. Unarmed men will be collected and put under a guard. An Officer from B.H.Q. will visit this Post and give instructions as to the disposal of the unarmed men.

Appendix 5.

Action by right and left companies in the event of the withdrawal by troops on either of our flanks.

1. Should No.3 Prov. G.G.Bn. withdraw to the line of resistance (Support Line) O.C. 909 Coy. will form a defensive flank in the C.T. in P 32 a

2. Should the troops on the right of 147 & 176 Coys. withdraw and render a withdrawal by these Coys. necessary, they will proceed along the trench running through V 14b & V 8d to B. H. Q. and report there.

These parties to be detailed at once, and reconnoitre the routes to the C.H.Q's concerned.

Appendix 6.

Notes on dispositions of Companies in the Line.

1. No.909 Coy. will include the right edge of the wood in V 3 a in its sector.

2. No.908 Coy. will have a detached post of 1 section at house in V 3 a central.

3. No.908 Coy. will have a detached post forward on the crest about V 4 a.o.5

4. No.147 Company will occupy sector from railway to C.T. (exclusive) one platoon in front & support lines, and one platoon in reserve.

5. No.176 Coy. will occupy sector from CT (excl) to road in V 14 d and 15 b excl. 1½ platoons in front and 1 platoon in reserve. & ½ platoon in C.T.

Appendix 7.

On Fighting Detachments being ordered to join the Garrison Guard Battalions the following will be the responsibility as regards their rations.

1. The Officer Commanding Labour Company is responsible that each man takes the unexpired portion of the current day's rations with him.

2. If rations for consumption on the following day have been delivered the Officer Commanding Labour Company is responsible that each man takes the rations for consumption on the following day with him; no transport will be available, and the men will have to carry this ration.

3. If rations for consumption on the following day have NOT been drawn from refilling points; The Supply Officer to the 190th Infantry Brigade is responsible that additional rations as under are issued to Garrison Guard Battalions, and the Sector Supply Officer is responsible that Labour Companies are under-issued as follows:-

No. of Labour Company.	No. of rations to be under-issued.	Garrison Guard Battalions.	No. of additional rations to be issued.
61	70	4th	150
93	80		
188	180	1st	180
55	213	3rd	213
147	95	2nd	227
176	132		

Appendix 3.

The methods being adopted to hold up the advance of the enemy in the enclosed country in Flanders should make full use of every building, hedge, or piece of broken ground etc. The defensive dispositions must be concealed.

Definite lines of defence should be dug in rear, but houses and buildings etc. which exist in front of these lines must be held to the last and must not be evacuated even when the flanks are turned. Every care must be taken to conceal men holding posts and no movements should be seen.

The enemy system of advance is to dribble forward into farm buildings, houses, broken ground etc. and to bring flanking fire to bear on our men occupying hastily dug and very visible trenches in the open.

Appendix 2.

Dispositions of Hotchkiss and Lewis Guns.

a. Hotchkiss Gun No.1.   On 903 Coy's front, approximately at P 33 a 0.0.

b. Hotchkiss Gun No.2.   On 903 Coy's front, approximately at V 3 c 5.5

c. Lewis Gun No.1.   On 147 Coy's front, approximately at V 9 c 8.4

d. Lewis Gun No.2.   On 178 Coy's front, approximately at V 15 a 5.7

In every case alternative emplacements must be sited by Coy. Commanders.

www.ingramcontent.com/pod-product-compliance
Lightning Source LLC
Chambersburg PA
CBHW081457160426
43193CB00013B/2516